She's the Art, She's the Artist -

A poetic guide to self-love, confidence and healing

Juhi Rathod

BookLeaf Publishing

India | USA | UK

Presentation by *BookLeaf Publishing*

Web: www.bookleafpub.com

E-mail: info@bookleafpub.com

ISBN: 9789363302235

First edition 2024

for the younger me who needed to hear these words

i am enough

you told me to go get thinner, to go become less
to shrink myself so i could finally fit in that dress
blamed all my problems on my increasing weight
till all i could provide to my own body was hate
my insecurities went through the roof
and all i could ever wish for
was my body to vanish like poof
you gratuitously advised with a wicked smile
to not get bigger
before every morsel of food i have ever loved
reduced to a trigger
i could not eat, no i couldn't, not in this state
it's like my stomach had closed its gate
tried all the cruel diets and thought
that maybe nothing would help my fate
thought that i would never be enough
convinced myself that the idea
of being happy in one's body
was all a big bluff
but little did i know that the day would finally come
when i would have the "perfect weight"
and you would stop being so hurtsome
i reduced to half my size
i would be enough for you now
one would think so, right?
but you said, and drumroll please
"you look so weak darling, are you alright?"
that's when realisation dawned on me

and i was shocked
no matter what i do
you are always going to be armed
with some hateful comment
you are never going to stop the torment
the hurtful words you say and your callous actions
i eventually understood are your own projections
no i do not hate you, but can muster only pity
now that i have promised myself
to never compromise on my self-respect and dignity
today, i celebrate and rejoice
as i have finally found my voice
to tell you how i don't care about your vile words
and your so called love that you claim is "tough"
because i truly love and appreciate myself now
and i am enough.

who you are

you are not your trauma
you are not your insecurities
you are not your past
you are not your fears
you are not what leaves you feeling aghast
you are not what happened to you
you are, rather
your kind spirit
so loving and true
you are your ability
to smile on days so unbearably blue
you are your favourite song
your goals, your dreams
the raw generosity that you bring along
you are the spark in your eyes
when you see the most gorgeous sunset
because, my love
how you define and perceive yourself
is ultimately your biggest asset.

forgive yourself

why is it that when it comes to everyone else
we forgive so easily
even when they have made a terrible mess?
why is it that when it comes to ourselves
we tend to forget there exists a word called
forgiveness?
you are a human being
a soul, the universe, the essence of life
isn't that thought so freeing?
why is it that we hate our past versions so?
why was i so cringe?
what was i on when i decided to get that fringe?
you were just as worthy back then too
you did your best with everything you knew
and all the resources you had access to
you do not need any more hate
you need
love
understanding
support
care
so i dare you to forgive yourself
because how can you expect someone else
to give you all that
when you cannot even give that to yourself?

time heals

moving on...
what is that? i asked
this was all i had ever known
something i was damn proud to get to call my own
each breath felt so liberating
like a butterfly soaring through the skies
in all its beauty and might
utterly majestic, colourful and bright
until i was pushed back into the cocoon of shame
dwindled to nothing but a pawn in your game
engulfed in the shadows
and threads of your remembrances
abiding my time in the prison of your deceptions
what does sunlight feel like? i asked
is this forever going to last?
one fine day the heavens smiled upon me
the dark clouds cleared
and a single ray of hope entered my cocoon with glee
aren't you tired? she asked
tired of wallowing in your self-pity?
you are not a victim no
you are a warrior, i wholeheartedly believe so
my tears dried and away went the shackles
i rose like a phoenix from the ashes
oh how empowering it feels
to finally breathe free
so trust me when i say that
time heals.

happiness

i kept looking for her
in that high-paying job
in that dream relationship
in the "perfect figure"
in flawless skin
i kept telling myself
i will find her
when i get all that
little did i know
she never existed in those things
that all this time
she lived within me
she was merely a choice
a choice to be happy today
a choice to be grateful today
no matter where you are
or where you aim to go
as the great professor dumbledore once said
that happiness can be found
even in the darkest of times
if one only remembers
to turn on the light.

i am worthy

for years in my life
i thought i needed to prove myself
to be worthy of respect
to be worthy of love
the pressure to be perfect
felt like burning over a scorching stove
constant comparison to other people
killed me from the inside
got caught up in a never ending race
it became impossible to look into the mirror
at myself, face-to-face
bended over backwards
just to gain petty, trivial approvals
years later i now perceive
i breathe and i am
therefore i am worthy.

self-love

8

how naive of me
to search for love and validation
externally
when the only thing
my soul has ever craved for
is love and acceptance
from within.

don't settle

you deserve a love that feels calm
a love that values you
one that presents the entire world to you in your palm
you deserve a love that makes you feel seen
a love that makes you feel heard
one that sweeps you off your feet
you deserve a love that makes you feel safe
a love that you can trust
one that even amidst stormy winds
will never rust
you deserve a love that is gentle
a love that is understanding
one that is willing to fight for you
and never leave you stranding
don't settle for something
that is less than what you deserve
simply because you feel alone
protect your energy
because the wait will be worth it
when you find someone
who will give you the world
and much more.

thank you

thank you
for making me realise
how big and beautiful
my heart is
thank you
for making me realise
how i need to protect it
even more fiercely
thank you
for making me realise
how deeply i care
how deeply i love
how deeply i cherish
how i always give my all
thank you for not loving me
the way i deserved
for it made me understand
what self-love is
in a way
i never did before.

don't tell me

11

don't tell me to be quiet
no don't tell me to agree with you
don't tell me to behave
don't tell me, "you better not argue"
you have only ever seen your own point of view
don't tell me i'm abnormal
don't tell me i'm problematic
don't tell me i'm such a mess
don't tell me i'm too much
because respectfully, you can go find less.

authenticity

isn't it so beautiful
how there is no one exactly like you
in this entire world?
how there is no one else
with your features
your personality
your habits
your energy
your heart
your mind
your potential
your kindness
your smile?
embrace your authenticity
appreciate the things
that make you, you
you were not put on this earth
to fit into
the stringent, narrow and foolish standards
set by this cruel society
you were not put on this earth
to be a curated version of somebody else
your purpose in life
is to instead follow your heart
and become the best version of yourself.

perspective

13

do not question
why is this happening to me?
instead, try to aim for
what can i learn from this to set myself free?
for the flower that blooms in adversity
is the prettiest of them all
standing so resilient and tall
overthinking is never effective
and most times, the only thing we truly need
is a change in perspective.

carnival

i still remember
the day i entered your carnival
it was the first of december
lost in the labyrinth of my first love
you led me to the ferris wheel
said it would be the best thing i'd ever feel
we rose to the top
before there came a sudden stop
oh how marvellous the view was
i began to bask in the feeling
i felt on top of the world
the sky was the ceiling
when we suddenly lost control
and hit the floor
the drop was agonising
the loss of the high
was utterly terrifying
sadness engulfed me
the chariot of my dreams
slammed into a tree
but up we shot
then down again
on edge was my heart
again and again
my anxiety knew no bounds
i don't want this, i thought
i don't want to feel this way
so lost and distraught

i deserve a love that is calm
like a tranquil sea
stable and
ever so trustworthy
is it too much
to want these things?
because i was so done and exhausted of being a prey
of your capricious demeanour
and unpredictable moodswings.

your words are powerful

can you fathom
how immensely powerful
we would be
if every self-deprecating word
we have ever told ourselves
was replaced with a kind one instead?

the art of letting go

one of the bravest things
you'll ever do
is letting go of things
that no longer serve you
it will feel as if
your heart is being
ripped out from your chest
but it will lead you
to what you truly deserve
to what is meant for you
it's not easy to let go
but it's also not easy
to stay and suffer
in the same toxic cycle
over and over again
letting go is freedom
letting go is the first step
in the journey called healing
in the journey called self-love
it's the ultimate form
of self-respect.

it's okay to feel

it's okay to feel sad
it's okay to feel angry
it's okay to feel hurt
it's okay to feel scared
it's okay to feel grief
it's okay to feel confused
it's okay to feel pain
these emotions
are not your enemies
but are in fact
your friends in disguise
trying to
communicate something with you
feeling them fully
is the only way
through them
the only way
to get to the other side
it's okay to feel them
it's okay to feel.

do you dare?

overwhelmed was my heart
when you voiced those three magical words
it's like the air was filled with honey
and the melody of euphonious birds
euphoria consumed me
and stripped me off the ground
my rational senses were nowhere to be found
your gentle touch caressed my cheek and assured me
you said i needn't be scared
the fact that you actually dared
dared to accept me completely and wholly
with all my craziness, quirks, insecurities,
the little things
all of which you noticed
and embraced so very closely
oh how you said so passionately that
i'm your one and only
i had to steady myself, my heart was beating so hard
slowly and cautiously,
i found myself putting down my guard
is this what love truly feels like
like a gust of fresh air in my lungs?
to trust someone so deeply that
there's no room for doubt?
to finally understand what céline dion sings about?
you looked into my eyes
then grabbed my hands
and urged me to say something, anything

it was impossible to form a single word
as i was still processing what i heard
in that moment, i knew i was hopelessly yours
you held my heart in your hands bare
stripped me of all my qualms
and voiced those three magical words when I asked
do you dare?

unstoppable

the most atrocious form of disservice
you can ever do to yourself
is harbouring self-doubt and limiting beliefs
about your unlimited being
you are so oblivious to the heaps of potential
that you store
encompassed in your majestic and beautiful core
do not be the one who just fell
be the one who got back up
do yourself the kindest favour
of believing in yourself
and putting confidence back on the shelf
do not stand in your own way
whatever you dream of
whatever you desire
it is possible
you are unstoppable.

overthinking

the basic purpose of our minds
is to think, sort and analyse
to devise solutions to our problems
then isn't it ironic
how nowadays
it unnecessarily creates most of them?
how true is the fact that
we suffer more in our heads
and our imaginations
than in reality?

validation

23

do not chase the idea of impressing someone else
which will eventually make you
lose yourself in the process
instead, how about pouring
all that energy into yourself?
because you are the only one you need to impress.

you are a rainbow

24

there will always be daylight after the storm
so don't be afraid of the pain
for the most beautiful rainbow is made
when sunlight meets the rain.